Champions Speak Out On

Baseball

COMPILED BY
Lance Wubbels

*"He trains my hands for battle, so that
my arms can bend a bow of bronze."*

—2 Samuel 22:35

Champions Speak Out on Baseball

Copyright © 2007 Lance Wubbels

ISBN 1-932458-26-3

Published by Bronze Bow Publishing LLC
2600 E. 26th Street, Minneapolis, MN 55406

You can reach us on the Internet at www.bronzebowpublishing.com

Literary development and cover/interior design by Koechel Peterson & Associates, Inc., Minneapolis, Minnesota.

Manufactured in the United States of America

The **Champions Speak Out** *Series*

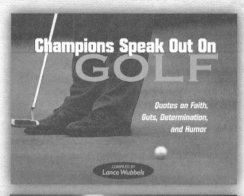

Champions Speak Out On GOLF

Quotes on Faith, Guts, Determination, and Humor

COMPILED BY
Lance Wubbels

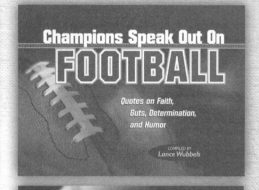

Champions Speak Out On FOOTBALL

Quotes on Faith, Guts, Determination, and Humor

COMPILED BY
Lance Wubbels

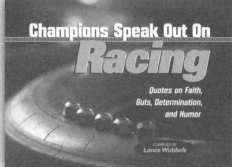

Champions Speak Out On Racing

Quotes on Faith, Guts, Determination, and Humor

COMPILED BY
Lance Wubbels

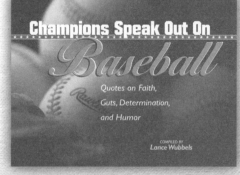

Champions Speak Out On Baseball

Quotes on Faith, Guts, Determination, and Humor

COMPILED BY
Lance Wubbels

Introduction

"Baseball mania has run its course. It has no future as a professional endeavor."
So proclaimed *The Cincinnati Gazette* in 1879. That prediction was spoken in all
seriousness, though history has proven it laughable. In the sandlots and the back
yards and the streets of America, boys and girls have never lost the "mania" or
passion for this unchanging game.

For over 150 years baseball has proven to be the timeless game for the ages. From generation to generation, its heroes have captured the hearts and minds of fans everywhere. What other game is as deeply embedded in the American way of life? From the early days of Cobb, Ruth, and Wagner to Williams, DiMaggio, Mantle, Robinson, and Koufax to Clemens, Johnson, and Rodriguez, the game of baseball has etched its indelible memories in our lives.

How else do you explain how a simple swatch of cowhide can become a lifelong friend? That faded glove of your childhood is packed with baseball memories that defy time. Or how do you explain why that old bat sits in your garage long after you've retired from the game? What magic does it hold from the past? Just because you never made it to the "big show" doesn't lessen the dreams it held.

The wonder of baseball has been captured in the words of its legendary players, managers, owners, and writers. The timeless truths they shared about their lives, often born out of years of struggle and long hours and fighting through injuries, not only capture our admiration but instruct us about life. If we're wise, we'll listen to their insights and wisdom and benefit from their example.

"You gotta be a man to play baseball for a living, but you gotta have a lot of little boy in you."

ROY CAMPANELLA

"When I was a boy growing up in Kansas, a friend of mine and I went fishing, and as we sat there in the warmth of a summer afternoon we talked about what we wanted to do when we grew up. I told him I wanted to be a real major league baseball player, a genuine professional like Honus Wagner. My friend said he'd like to be the president of the United States. Neither of us got our wish."

PRESIDENT DWIGHT D. EISENHOWER

"Baseball is 90 percent mental. The other half is physical."

YOGI BERRA

"Sometimes in this game
it's as good to be lucky as
it is to be good."
VIDA BLUE

"*A hot dog at the ballpark is better than steak at the Ritz.*"

HUMPHREY BOGART

"**You can't have a can when you**

miracle every day–except you get great pitching."

CASEY STENGEL

"People ask me what I do in winter when there's no baseball. I'll tell you what I do. I stare out the window and wait for spring."

ROGER HORNSBY

"Catching is much like managing. Managers don't really win games, but they can lose plenty of them. The same way with catching. If you're doing a quality job, you should be almost anonymous."

BOB BOONE

"People who write about spring training not being necessary have never tried to throw a baseball."

SANDY KOUFAX

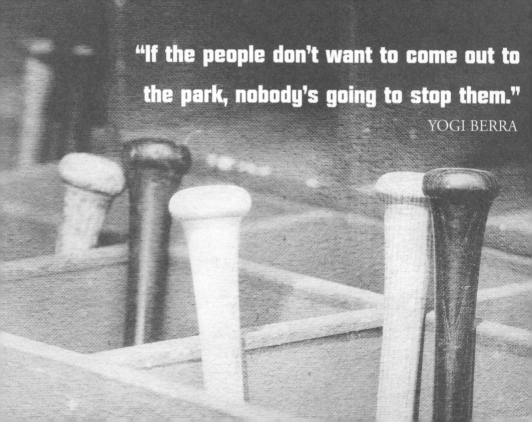

"If the people don't want to come out to the park, nobody's going to stop them."

YOGI BERRA

"Baseball is a simple game. If you have good players, and if you keep them in the right frame of mind, then the manager is a success. The players make the manager; it's never the other way."

SPARKY ANDERSON

"The lethargy and dull despair that accompany a losing streak can't be dismissed completely except by winning."

JIM BROSNAN

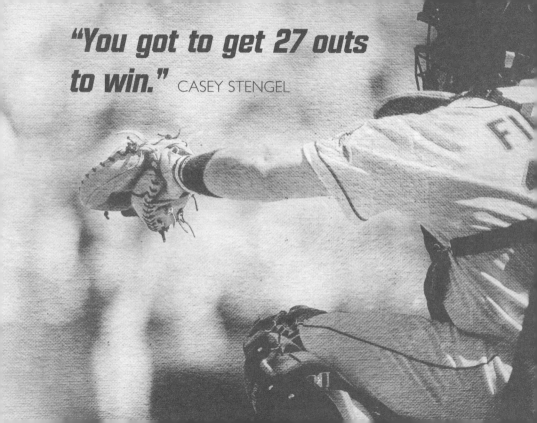

"You got to get 27 outs to win." CASEY STENGEL

"More than any other American sport, baseball creates the magnetic, addictive illusion that it can almost be understood."

THOMAS BOSWELL

"How to hit home runs: I swing as hard as I can, and I try to swing right through the ball. The harder you grip the bat, the more you can swing it through the ball, the farther the ball will go. I swing big, with everything I've got. I hit big or I miss big. I like to live as big as I can."

BABE RUTH

"Any time you think you have the game conquered, the game will turn around and punch you right in the nose."

MIKE SCHMIDT

"Sweat is the greatest solvent for problems."

BRANCH RICKEY

"The great thing about baseball is that there's a crisis every day."

GABE PAUL

"The greatest teacher is visualization—seeing others do it and aspiring to their level."

TONY KUBEK

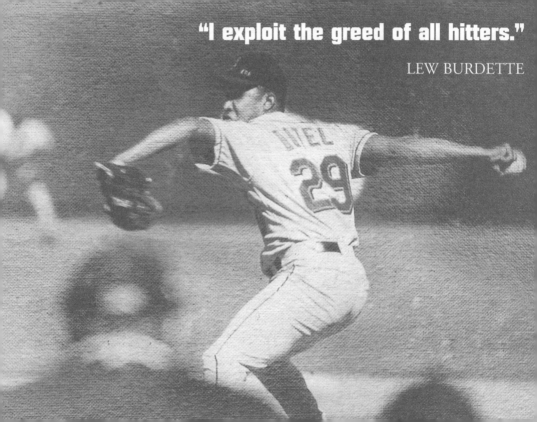

"I exploit the greed of all hitters."

LEW BURDETTE

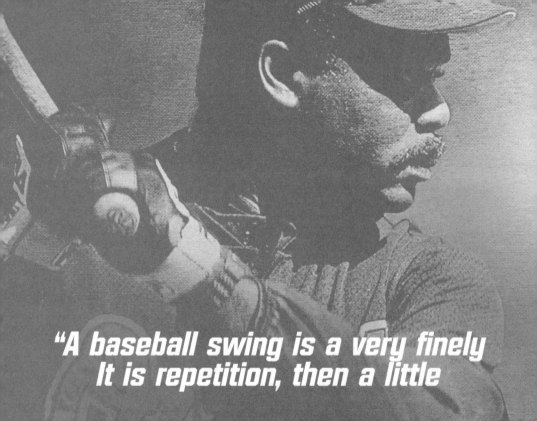

"A baseball swing is a very finely
It is repetition, then a little

"All winter long, I can't wait for baseball. It gets you back to doing the stuff you love and makes you wish the youthfulness of life could stay with you forever."

TOMMY JOHN

"Baseball is a game where a curve is an optical illusion, a screwball can be a pitch or a person, stealing is legal, and you can spit anywhere you like except in the umpire's eye or on the ball."

JIM MURRAY

tuned instrument.
more after that." REGGIE JACKSON

★
★
★

"*The practical joke is the psychiatry of baseball.*"

RON LUCIANO

"A full mind is an empty bat."

BRANCH RICKEY

"If you don't catch the ball, you catch the bus."

ROCKY BRIDGES

"If I had played my career hitting singles like Pete [Rose], I'd wear a dress."

MICKEY MANTLE

"I don't think about goals and records. Competition is what keeps me playing—the psychological warfare of matching skill against skill and wit against wit. If you're successful in what you do over a period of time, you'll start approaching records, but that's not what you're playing for. You're playing to challenge and be challenged."

LOU BROCK

"When you're a professional, you come back, no matter what happened the day before."

BILLY MARTIN

"My idea of the height of conceit would be a political speaker who would go on the air when the World Series is on."

WILL ROGERS

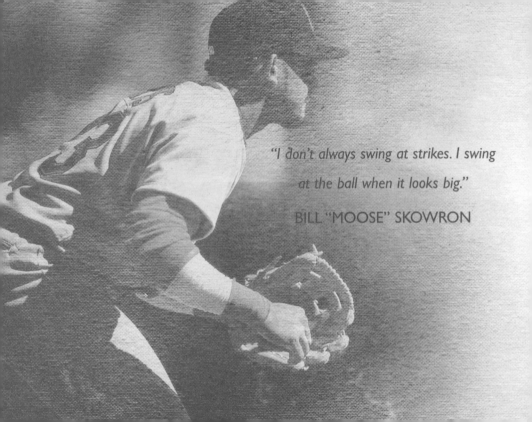

"I don't always swing at strikes. I swing at the ball when it looks big."

BILL "MOOSE" SKOWRON

"Anybody who says he isn't nervous or excited in a World Series is either crazy or a liar."

ROGERS HORNSBY

"In baseball, my theory is to strive for consistency, not to worry about the 'numbers.' If you dwell on statistics, you get shortsighted; if you aim for consistency, the numbers will be there in the end. My job isn't to strike guys out; it's to get them out, sometimes by striking them out."

TOM SEAVER

★ ★ ★

"They give you a round
bat and they throw you a
round ball. And they tell
you to hit square."

WILLIE STARGELL

"How good was Stan Musial? He was good enough to take your breath away."

VIN SCULLY

"Don't look back. Something might be gaining on you."

SATCHEL PAIGE

"Control does not mean throwing strikes every time. It means throwing where a particular hitter will not hit it."

JUAN MARICHAL

"*Baseball is for every boy a good, wholesome sport. It brings him out of the close confines of the schoolroom. It takes the stoop from his shoulders and puts hard honest muscle all over his frame. It rests his eyes, strengthens his lungs, and teaches him self-reliance and courage. Every mother ought to rejoice when her boy says he is on the school or college nine.*"

WALTER CAMP

"You can learn little from victory. You can learn everything from defeat."

CHRISTY MATHEWSON

"Take care of your body.
You only get one."

MICKEY MANTLE

"Baseball is a game
of inches."

BRANCH RICKEY

"I don't make speeches. I just let my bat speak for me in the summertime."

HONUS WAGNER

"The more the challenge, the more mental and spiritual strength you can come up with, and the stronger you're going to be in some other situation, away from the ballpark. Baseball is part of life, maybe only a small part, but the important thing is what you overcome inside yourself."

GEORGE FOSTER

"I like to play happy.

Baseball is a fun game, and I love it."

WILLIE MAYS

"The fans like to see home runs, and we have

assembled a pitching staff for their enjoyment."

CLARK GRIFFIN

"Keep hammering away."

HANK AARON

"You spend a good piece of your life gripping a baseball,

and it turns out it was the other way around all the time."

JIM BOUTON

"Mickey Mantle can hit just as good right-handed as he can left-handed. He's just naturally amphibious."

YOGI BERRA

"Show me a guy who's afraid to look bad, and I'll show you a guy you can beat every time."

LOU BROCK

"I don't think any player ever gets tired when he's hitting [well]. The ball looks bigger than usual and the fielders seem spaced way out. When you're not hitting, the ball looks smaller and it seems like even the umpires have gloves and you can't find a hole."

PETE ROSE

★
★
★

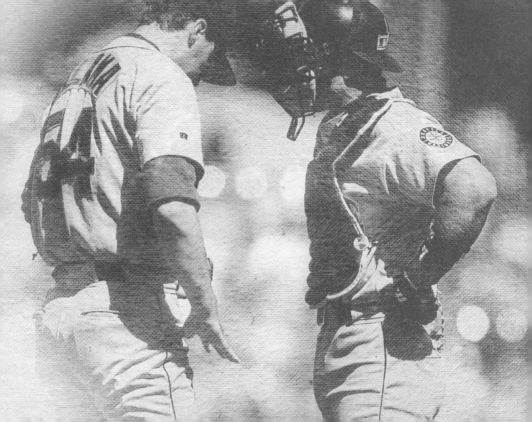

"Under pressure, you want to be at peace with yourself. You want your energy to flow, not feel knotted. You don't want to be too sharp. You don't want to be too flat. You just want to be natural."

WILLIE STARGELL

"I never want to quit playing ball. They'll have to cut this uniform off me to get me out of it."

ROY CAMPANELLA

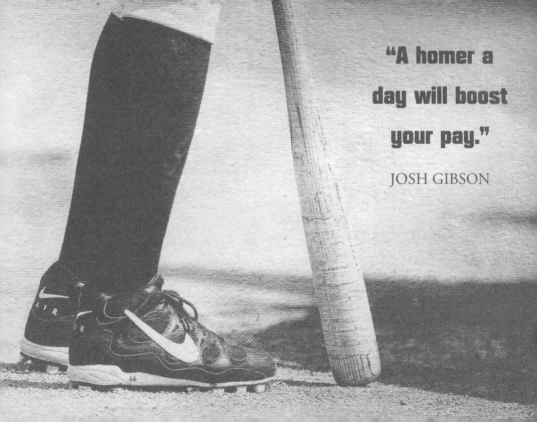

"A homer a day will boost your pay."

JOSH GIBSON

"I've had a lifelong ambition to be a professional baseball player, but nobody would sign me."

PRESIDENT GERALD FORD

★ ★ ★

"Ya gotta believe."

TUG McGRAW

★ ★ ★

"[Rickey Henderson] can run anytime he wants. I'm giving him the red light."

YOGI BERRA

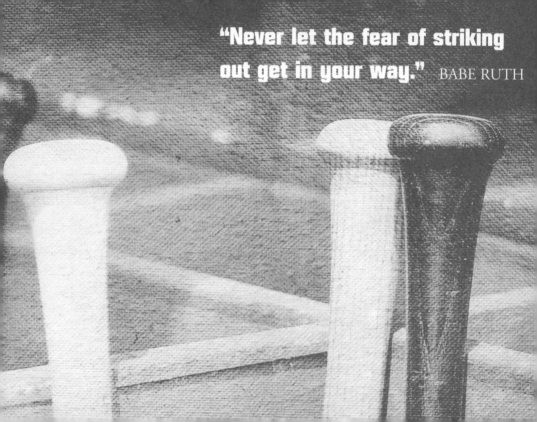

"Never let the fear of striking out get in your way." BABE RUTH

"If God wanted football to be played in the spring, he would not have invented baseball."

SAM RUTIGLIANO

"Any umpire who claims he has never missed a play is...well, an umpire."

RON LUCIANO

"Baseball is like this. Have one good year and you can fool them for five more, because for five more years they expect you to have another good one."

FRANK FRISCH

"A life isn't significant except for its impact on other lives."

JACKIE ROBINSON

"A team is where a boy can prove his courage on his own.

A gang is where a coward goes to hide."

MICKEY MANTLE

"Ninety feet between bases is perhaps as close as man has ever come to perfection."

RED SMITH

"The man with the ball is responsible for what happens to the ball."

BRANCH RICKEY

"The best pitch looks like a strike...but isn't."

WARREN SPAHN

"There are bad days and good days, bad months and good months, bad years and good years. If you lose, pick yourself up and carry on. That's baseball. And that's life."

TIM McCARVER

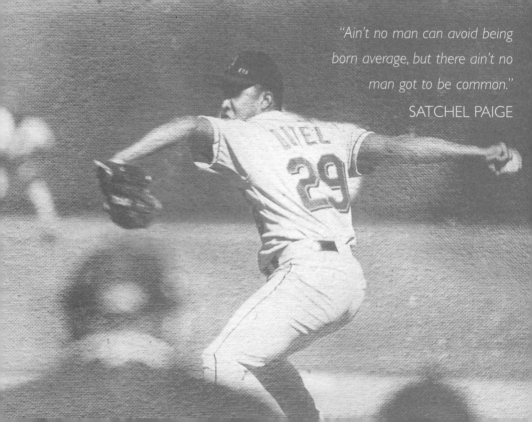

"Ain't no man can avoid being born average, but there ain't no man got to be common."

SATCHEL PAIGE

"The romance of baseball…is in its capacity for stirring fantasy. We are never too old or too bothered to see ourselves wrapping up a World Series victory with a homer in the final inning of the seventh game."

RON FIMRITE

"Batting is a problem you solve over and over again, but never master."

TY COBB

"Success is being truly happy at what you do."

TOMMY LASORDA

"I never threw an illegal pitch. The trouble is, once in a while I toss one that ain't never been seen by this generation."

SATCHEL PAIGE

"Any ballplayer who doesn't sign autographs for little kids ain't an American. He's a communist."

ROGERS HORNSBY

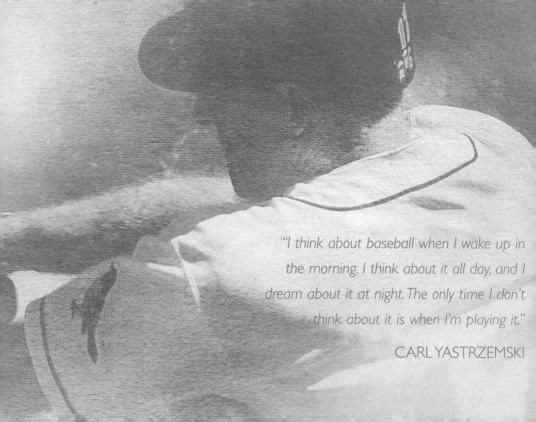

"I think about baseball when I wake up in the morning. I think about it all day, and I dream about it at night. The only time I don't think about it is when I'm playing it."

CARL YASTRZEMSKI

★ ★ ★

"Sweat plus sacrifice equals success."

CHARLIE FINLEY

"I'm not concerned with your liking or disliking me.

All I ask is that you respect me as a human being."

JACKIE ROBINSON

"You just can't beat the person who never gives up."

BABE RUTH

"There is nothing owed to you."

BILL VEECK

"If you come to a fork in the road, take it."

YOGI BERRA

"It was impossible to watch him at bat without experiencing an emotion. I have seen hundreds of ballplayers at the plate, and none of them managed to convey the message of impending doom to a pitcher that Babe Ruth did with the cock of his head, the position of his legs, and the little gentle waving of the bat, feathered in his two big paws."

PAUL GALLICO

"Most managers think winning creates chemistry. I think chemistry creates winning."

SPARKY ANDERSON

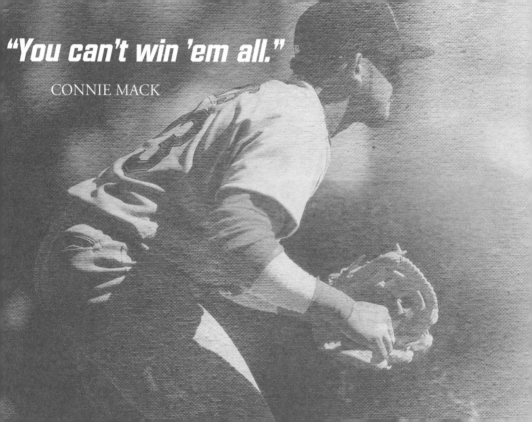

"You can't win 'em all."

CONNIE MACK

"The players are too serious. They don't have any fun anymore. They come to camp with a financial adviser, and they read the stock market page before the sports pages. They concern themselves with statistics rather than simply playing the game and enjoying it for what it is. Sure, I've got a job to do, but I also try to give them a little humor. They play better when they relax, and when they play better I can relax."

ROCKY BRIDGES

"Good pitching always stops good hitting and vice versa."

BOB VEALE

"The greatest players of all time are the ones with zest."

BRANCH RICKEY

"You can't win 'em in the clubhouse."

JIM BROSNAN

"You would be amazed how many important outs you can get by working the count down to where the hitter is sure you're going to throw to his weakness, and then throw to his power instead."

WHITEY FORD

"A hitter's impatience is the pitcher's biggest advantage."

PETE ROSE

"The game of ball is glorious."

WALT WHITMAN

"You gotta keep the ball off the fat part of the bat."

SATCHEL PAIGE

"Most ball games are lost, not won."

CASEY STENGAL

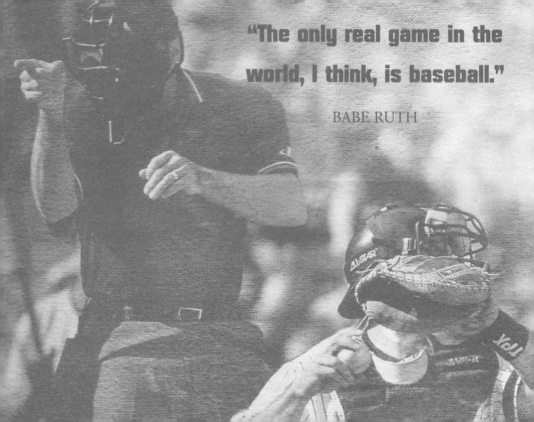

"The only real game in the world, I think, is baseball."

BABE RUTH

"Pitching is really just an internal struggle between the pitcher and his stuff. If my curve ball is breaking and I'm throwing it where I want, then the batter is irrelevant."

STEVE STONE

"You're never as good as you look when you're winning, and you're never as bad as you look when you're losing."

EARL WEAVER

"Close don't count in baseball. Close only counts in horseshoes and grenades."

FRANK ROBINSON

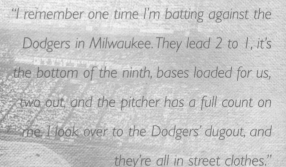

"Hello again, everybody. It's a *bee-yooo-tiful* day for baseball."

HARRY CARAY

★ ★ ★

"I remember one time I'm batting against the Dodgers in Milwaukee. They lead 2 to 1, it's the bottom of the ninth, bases loaded for us, two out, and the pitcher has a full count on me. I look over to the Dodgers' dugout, and they're all in street clothes."

BOB UECKER

"It ain't over 'til
it's over."

YOGI BERRA

"Baseball is continuity: pitch to pitch, inning to inning,

game to game, series to series, season to season."

ERNIE HARWELL

"They throw the ball, I hit it; they hit the ball, I catch it."

WILLIE MAYS

"The ballplayer who loses his head, who can't keep his cool,

is worse than no ballplayer at all."

LOU GEHRIG

"The best thing about baseball is that you can do something about yesterday tomorrow."

MANNY TRILLO

"There is always some kid who may be seeing me for the first or last time. I owe him my best."

JOE DiMAGGIO

"It's a pretty sure thing that a player's bat is what speaks loudest when it's contract time, but there are moments when the glove has the last word."

BROOKS ROBINSON

"Learn the fundamentals.

Study and work at the game as if it were a science.

Keep in top physical condition.

Make yourself as effective as possible.

Get the desire to win.

Keeping in the best physical condition and having an intense

spirit to succeed is the combination for winning games."

TY COBB

"It ain't braggin' if you can do it."

DIZZY DEAN

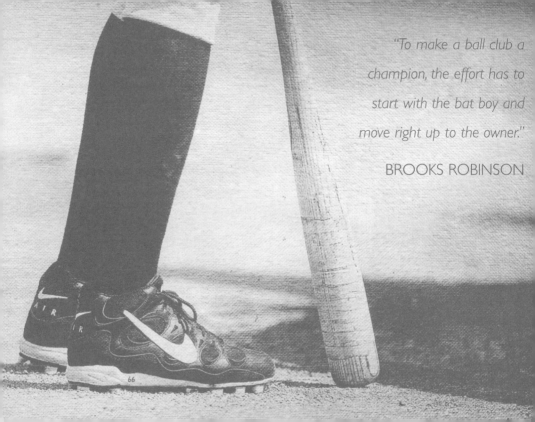

"To make a ball club a champion, the effort has to start with the bat boy and move right up to the owner."

BROOKS ROBINSON

"If a man can beat you, walk him."

SATCHEL PAIGE

"It's better to throw a theoretically poorer pitch wholeheartedly than to throw the so-called right pitch with a feeling of doubt."

SANDY KOUFAX

★ ★ ★

"Success doesn't just happen. You've got to make it happen."

JOE McCARTHY

"Baseball gives you every chance to be great. Then it puts every pressure on you to prove that you haven't got what it takes. It never takes away the chance, and it never eases up on the pressure."

JOE GARAGIOLA

"Baseball is like church. Many attend, but few understand."

WES WESTRUM

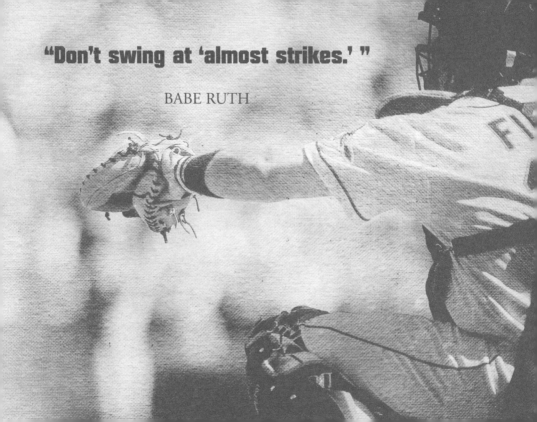

"Don't swing at 'almost strikes.'"

BABE RUTH

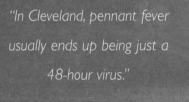

"In Cleveland, pennant fever usually ends up being just a 48-hour virus."

FRANK ROBINSON

"Baseball is a game that allows us to stay young at heart."

TOMMY JOHN

"I'm just a ballplayer with one ambition, and that is to give all I've got to help my ball club win. I've never played any other way."

JOE DiMAGGIO

"Fundamentals are the most valuable tools a player can possess. Bunt the ball into the ground. Hit the cutoff man. Take the extra base. Learn the fundamentals."

DICK WILLIAMS

"Work at what doesn't come easy to you."

TY COBB

"Bob Gibson's the luckiest pitcher I've ever seen, because he always picks the nights to pitch when the other team doesn't score any runs."

TIM McCARVER

"You can't tell how much spirit a team has until it starts losing."

ROCKY COLAVITO

"Self-confidence is the hallmark of a champion—any champion."

GRANTLAND RICE

"I made up my mind, but I made it up both ways."

CASEY STENGEL

"Slumps are like a soft bed. They're easy to get into and hard to get out of."

JOHNNY BENCH

"When I pick up the ball and it feels nice and light and small, I know I'm going to have a good day. But if I pick it up and it's big and heavy, I know I'm liable to get into a little trouble."

BOB FELLER

"A curve ball is not something you can pick up overnight. It took me years to perfect mine."

BOB GIBSON

"There are two theories on hitting the knuckleball.

Unfortunately, neither one works."

CHARLIE LAU

"Uniforms change, but friendships don't."

WHITEY HERZOG

"If you ain't got a bullpen, you ain't got nothin'."

YOGI BERRA

"Every day is a new opportunity. You can build on yesterday's success or put its failures behind and start over. That's the way life is, with a new game every day, and that's the way baseball is."

BOB FELLER

"It breaks your heart. It is designed to break your heart. The game begins in the spring, when everything else begins again, and it blossoms in the summer, filling the afternoons and evenings, and then as soon as the chill rains come, it stops and leaves you to face the fall alone."

BART GIAMATTI

"When you're through learning, you're through."

VERNON LAW

"The wildest pitch is not necessarily the one that goes back to the screen. It can also be the one that goes right down the middle."

SANDY KOUFAX

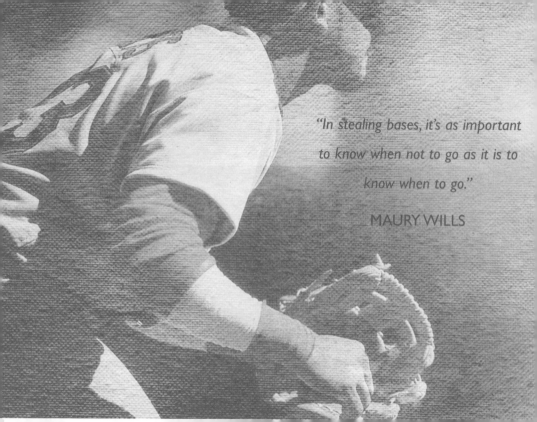

"In stealing bases, it's as important to know when not to go as it is to know when to go."

MAURY WILLS

"You can't have a long, successful career without a positive attitude."

NOLAN RYAN

"It may sound silly, but I don't hear a thing when I'm up at bat. Someone can be standing and hollering right by the dugout, but I don't hear it. I'm concentrating on the pitcher. I don't worry about what's happening in the stands."

HANK AARON

"Just give me 25 guys on the last year of their contracts; I'll win a pennant every year."

SPARKY ANDERSON

"An athlete needs God-given ability, but discipline achieves success."

FERGUSON JENKINS

"Trying to sneak a pitch past Hank Aaron is like trying to sneak the sunrise past a rooster."

JOE ADCOCK

"Keep your eyes clear and hit 'em where they ain't."

WEE WILLIE KEELER

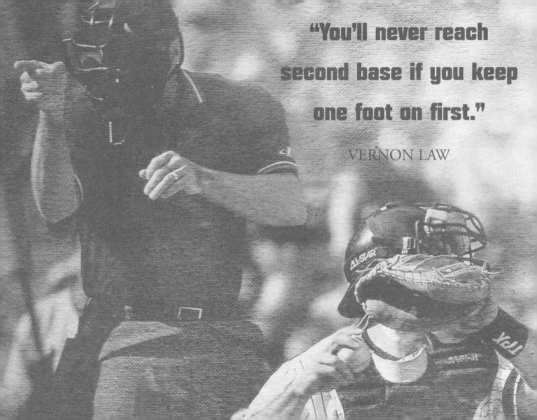

"You'll never reach second base if you keep one foot on first."

VERNON LAW

"These moments are the soul of baseball: the ball perfectly hit, perfectly caught, or perfectly thrown. We can unwrap the moments later, when it's quiet, and enjoy them all over again."

ALISON GORDON

"Baseball is a ballet without music.

Drama without words.

A carnival without Kewpie dolls."

ERNIE HARWELL

"It's going, going,
gone."

MEL ALLEN

"Catching a fly ball is a pleasure, but knowing what to do with it after you catch it is a business."

TOMMY HENRICH

"Hitting is timing. Pitching is upsetting timing."

WARREN SPAHN

"When you watch baseball at its best, there's a tendency to forget the real world."

MICKEY MANTLE

"Look at misfortune the same way you look at success: don't panic.

Do your best and forget the consequences."

WALTER ALSTON

"Baseball is our national game."

PRESIDENT CALVIN COOLIDGE

"Being traded is like celebrating your 100th birthday. It might not be the happiest

occasion in the world, but consider the alternatives."

JOE GARAGIOLA

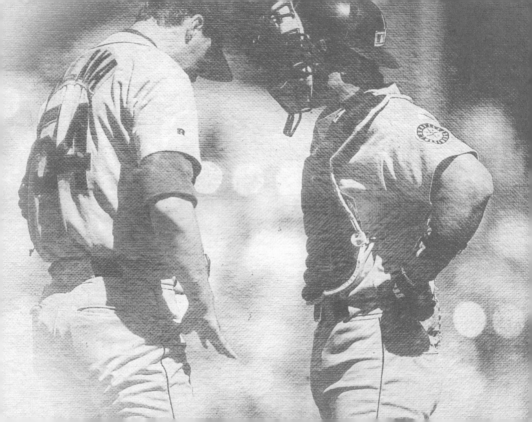

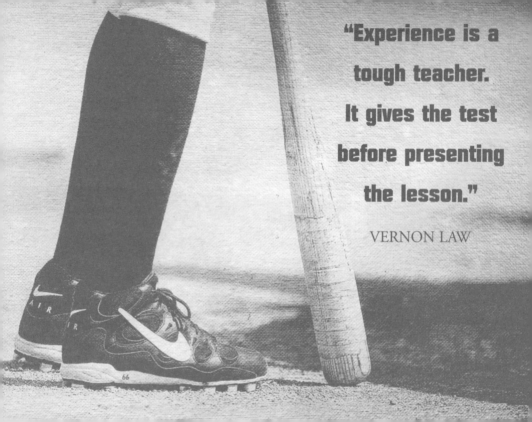

"Experience is a tough teacher. It gives the test before presenting the lesson."

VERNON LAW

"Statistics are used like a drunk uses a lamppost—for support, not illumination."

VIN SCULLY

"The difference between the possible and the impossible lies in a person's determination."

TOMMY LASORDA

"Problems are the price you pay for progress."

BRANCH RICKEY

"Make optimism a way of life."

BROOKS ROBINSON

"Some teams never win. They've got four or five guys who never care about anything. They don't want the grind of the full six months. As soon as things start to go bad, they crack and just go for themselves. Talent is one thing. Being able to go from spring to October is another."

SPARKY ANDERSON

"How old would you be if you didn't know how old you was?"

SATCHEL PAIGE

"I don't want to achieve immortality by making the Hall of Fame.
I want to achieve immortality by not dying."

LEO DUROCHER

"Has anyone ever satisfactorily explained why the bad hop is always the last one?"

HANK GREENWALD

"That's the true harbinger of spring, not crocuses or swallows returning to
Capistrano, but the sound of a bat on the ball."

BILL VEECK

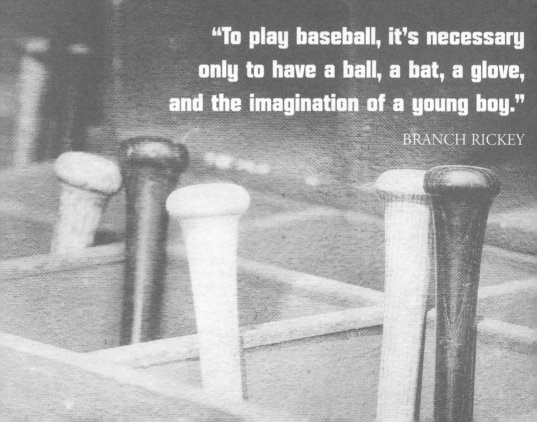

"To play baseball, it's necessary only to have a ball, a bat, a glove, and the imagination of a young boy."

BRANCH RICKEY

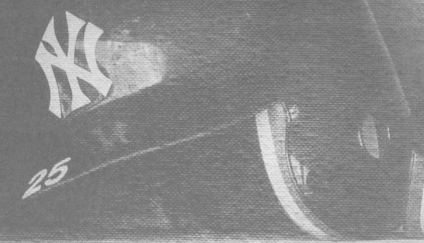

"*Generate happiness within yourself.*"

ERNIE BANKS

"Dad always said, 'Practice, practice, practice.' Dad was right. Practice paid off."

MICKEY MANTLE

★ ★ ★

"A can-do mentality is a pitcher's best friend."

NOLAN RYAN

"All good balls to hit are strikes, though not all strikes are good balls to hit."

DAVE WINFIELD

"You have to get your uniform dirty."

PETE ROSE

"My advice to third basemen? Get your glove down on the ground and in position to field the ball."

BROOKS ROBINSON

"We have deep depth."

YOGI BERRA

"We want pitchers who aren't happy to leave the game. I'd rather have a pitcher come in and kick the water cooler than someone who is resigned to failure."

ROGER CRAIG

"You can't be afraid to make errors. No one ever masters baseball or conquers it. You only challenge it."

LOU BROCK

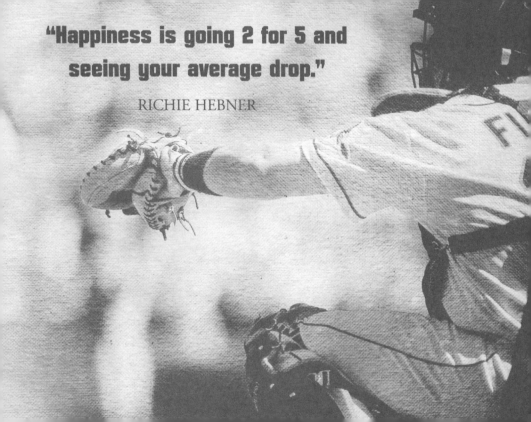

"Happiness is going 2 for 5 and seeing your average drop."

RICHIE HEBNER

"All you have to do is pick up a baseball. It begs to you: throw me. If you took a year to design an object to hurl, you'd end up with that little spheroid: small enough to nestle in your fingers but big enough to have some heft, lighter than a rock but heavier than a hunk of wood. Its even, neat stitching, laced into the leather's slippery white surface, gives your fingers a purchase. A baseball was made to throw. It's almost irresistible."

DAVE DRAVECKY

"Babe Ruth struck out 1,330 times."

NEW YORK CITY GRAFFITI

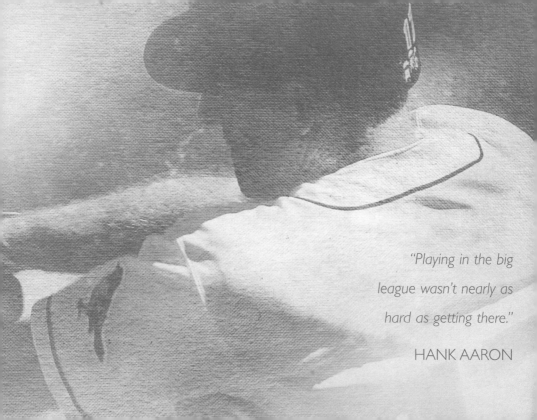

"Playing in the big league wasn't nearly as hard as getting there."

HANK AARON

"Kiss It Goodbye."

BOB PRINCE

"*Don't try to be somebody you're not. They tried to make me into the mold of Babe Ruth, but I didn't want to fit anyone's mold.*"

ROGER MARIS

"Don't tell them what you did in the past; tell them what you are going to do in the future."

STAN MUSIAL

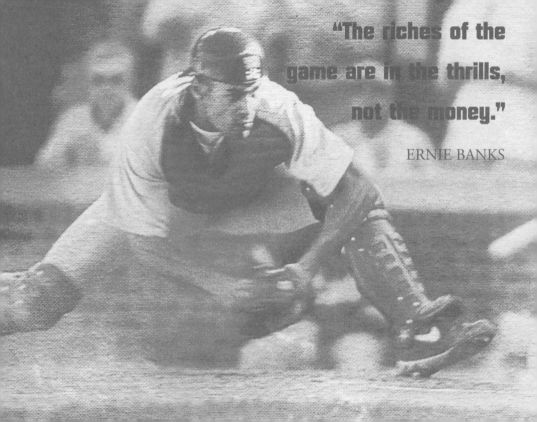

"The riches of the game are in the thrills, not the money."

ERNIE BANKS

"Never give the other guy the satisfaction of hearing you squawk."

TY COBB

★ ★ ★

"The trick is growing up without growing old."

CASEY STENGEL

★ ★ ★

"You can always take what you have and make it better."

TED WILLIAMS

"Baseball is a lot like life. The line drives are caught, the squibbers go for base hits. It's an unfair game."

ROD KANEHL

"You cannot hit a home run by bunting. You have to step up there and take a cut at the ball. Never be more scared of the enemy than you think he is of you."

PRESIDENT DWIGHT D. EISENHOWER

"An outfielder who throws behind a runner is locking the barn door after the horse is stolen."

JOE McCARTHY

"Take nothing for granted

"Prefer the errors of enthusiasm to the complacency of wisdom."

BRANCH RICKEY

"Baseball is a game to be savored rather than taken in gulps."

BILL VEECK

"Get a good ball to hit."

ROGERS HORNSBY

in baseball."

HARRY PULLIAM

"Gentlemen, he was out…because I said he was out."

BILL KLEM

"Think. Don't just swing. Think about the pitcher, what he threw you last time up, his best pitch, who's up next. Think."

TED WILLIAMS

"A true champion is one who dedicates himself to give his best at all times. The only thing God ever expects from any of us is to give it our very best."

GARY CARTER

"All my life I tried to be honest with people.

I wish I had been a little more honest with myself."

MICKEY MANTLE

"Slump? I ain't in no slump. I just ain't hitting."

YOGI BERRA

"When they operated on my arm, I asked them to put in Koufax's fastball.

They did. But it turned out to be Mrs. Koufax."

TOMMY JOHN

"It's a great day
for a ballgame;
let's play two."

ERNIE BANKS

"If you're afraid, you'll never do the job."

BILL MAZEROSKI

"The saddest day of the year is the day baseball season ends."

TOMMY LASORDA

"You don't save a pitcher for tomorrow. Tomorrow it may rain."

LEO DUROCHER

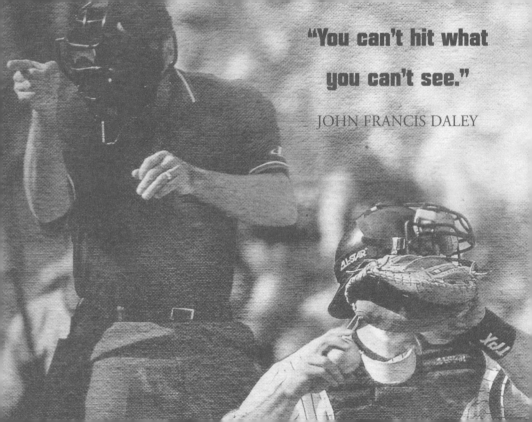

"You can't hit what
you can't see."

JOHN FRANCIS DALEY

"Managing is like holding a dove in your hand. Squeeze too hard and you kill it, not hard enough and it flies away."

TOMMY LASORDA

"They say you have to be good to be lucky, but I think you have to be lucky to be good."

RICO CARTY

"If I'd known I was gonna pitch a no-hitter today, I would have gotten a haircut."

BO BELINSKY

"*The most cowardly thing in the world is blaming mistakes upon the umpires. Too many managers strut around on the field trying to manage the umpires instead of their teams.*"

BILL KLEM

★ ★ ★

"Everything is possible to him who dares."

A. G. SPALDING

"You've got to be careful if you don't know where you're going, because you might not get there."

YOGI BERRA

"Tragedy offers you a different perspective on life. There are far more important things than wins and losses."

TOMMY JOHN

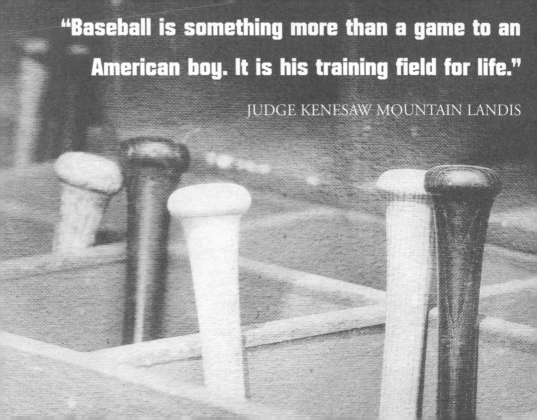

"Baseball is something more than a game to an American boy. It is his training field for life."

JUDGE KENESAW MOUNTAIN LANDIS

"Keep your alibis to yourself."

CHRISTY MATHEWSON

"Losing streaks are funny. If you lose at the beginning, you get off to a bad start. If you lose in the middle of the season, you're in a slump. If you lose at the end, you're choking."

GENE MAUCH

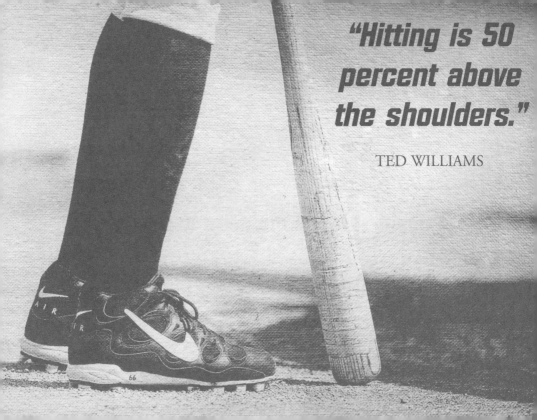

"Hitting is 50 percent above the shoulders."

TED WILLIAMS

★
★
★

"It really doesn't matter who is standing in the batter's box if you can keep the focus on the mitt and just play catch with your catcher. There are games when I don't even see anybody step in the batter's box."

ANDY PETTITTE

"Pitchers did me a favor when they knocked me down. It made me more determined."

FRANK ROBINSON

"Anybody with ability can play in the big leagues. But to be able to trick people year in and year out the way I did—I think that's a much greater feat."

BOB UECKER

"I've had a lot of individual success in my life that didn't fully satisfy me. There was always a void. Is that all there is when you hit .300? Is that all there is when you're an All-Star? You come to realize that what really is important is that unifying factor with our Savior and Lord, Jesus Christ. It puts everything into perspective."

LOU PINELLA

"If what you did yesterday still looks big to you, you haven't done much today."

CHIEF BENDER

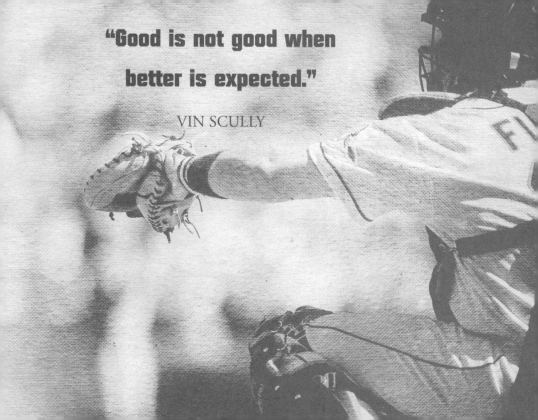

"Good is not good when better is expected."

VIN SCULLY

"Challenging a hitter is part of the game. You've got to do that if you want to be a successful pitcher in the big leagues."

PEDRO MARTINEZ

"If you aren't happy in one place, chances are pretty good you won't be happy in another place."

ERNIE BANKS

"It's dangerous for an athlete to believe his own publicity, good or bad."

BOB UECKER

"Not making the baseball team at West Point was one of the greatest disappointments of my life, maybe the greatest."

PRESIDENT DWIGHT D. EISENHOWER

"If you throw a lot of guys together—superstars—a lot of times it's not going to equate to victories. You have to have certain pieces that fit together. You need guys who are going to do the little intangibles that aren't in the box score."

WALT WEISS

"You observe a lot by watching."

YOGI BERRA

"Never surrender
opportunity to
security."

BRANCH RICKEY

"If you have skills, it's easy to play the game. But it's what you do off the field that dictates whether or not you're a star."

WILLIE MAYS

"Baseball is not the player's game or the manager's game.

It's not the owner's game. It's the fan's game."

SPARKY ANDERSON

"The space between the white lines–that's my office. That's where I conduct my business."

EARLY WYNN

"For when that One Great Scorer comes to mark against your name,

He writes—not that you won or lost—but how you played the game."

GRANTLAND RICE

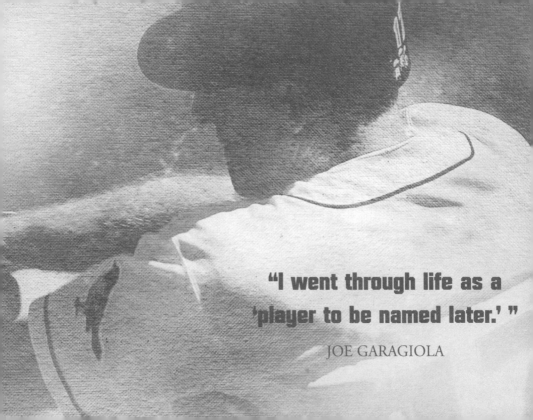

"I went through life as a
'player to be named later.' "

JOE GARAGIOLA

"You play through pressure—whether it's from fans, family, or people back home. It was said to me when I was a lot younger that 'excellence can only be measured by yourself.' You can't rely on other people to tell you how good or how bad you are."

TODD WALKER

"We're not exactly hitting the ball off the cover."

YOGI BERRA

"I have an Alka-Seltzer bat.
You know, 'Plop, plop, fizz, fizz.'
When the pitchers see me
walking up there, they say,
'Oh, what a relief it is.'"

ANDY VAN SLYKE

"It never ceased to amaze me how many of baseball's wounds are self-inflicted."

BILL VEECK

"You know I signed with the Milwaukee Braves for $3,000. That bothered my dad at the time, because he didn't have that kind of dough to pay out. But eventually he scraped it up."

BOB UECKER

"I don't look for excuses. Anybody who thinks that they're not going to suffer some type of tribulation, they're just kidding themselves. There were a lot of times when it would have been easier to go ahead and quit. But it's all about perseverance."

GARY GAETTI

★ ★ ★

"More men fail
through lack of
purpose than lack
of talent."

BILLY SUNDAY

"The key to my success as an athlete is the pressure the Lord has taken off of me—the pressure of success and of winning. Success to me now is working hard and doing my best, whereas success used to be just the numbers that are put up on the board. I just focus on going out there and doing my best."

OREL HERSHISER

"A pitcher's got to be good and he's got to be lucky to get a no-hit game."

CY YOUNG

"I couldn't see well enough to play when I was a boy, so they gave me a special job— they made me the umpire."

PRESIDENT HARRY TRUMAN

"I think God has given me the ability to play baseball. It's my responsibility to work hard and do the best job I can. But as far as results, and what's going to happen in the future, it's really given me peace to know that God has a plan for me. He's in control."

JOHN OLERUD

"I may not be the best pitcher in the world, but I sure out-cutes 'em."

SATCHEL PAIGE

"The secret of managing a club is to keep the five guys who hate you from the five who are undecided."

CASEY STENGAL

"The biggest thing I've found in hitting is not to get discouraged and change something that gets you completely messed up—even though the tendency is often overwhelming. But you just can't do it and survive. I was a lousy hitter in May doing exactly the same things that made me a great hitter in June."

CARL YASTRZEMSKI

"The other team could make trouble

for us if they win."
YOGI BERRA

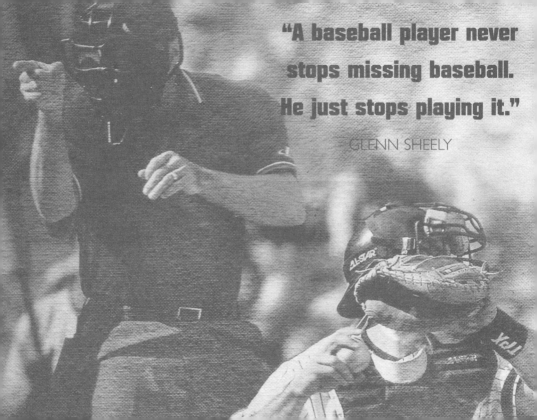

"A baseball player never stops missing baseball. He just stops playing it."

GLENN SHEELY

"Baseball is the only field of endeavor where a man can succeed three times out of ten and be considered a good performer."

TED WILLIAMS

"Take time to thank everyone who has helped you along the way."

BROOKS ROBINSON

LANCE WUBBELS is the Vice President of Literary Acquisition and Development at Bronze Bow Publishing. He has authored several fiction and non-fiction books, including two of Hallmark's bestselling gift books, *If Only I Knew* and *Dance While You Can*. He has also written the Angel Award-winning novel *One Small Miracle* and the Gold Medallion-winning books *To a Child Love Is Spelled T-I-M-E* and *In His Presence*. And he has compiled and edited twenty-five other books that are published under his name.

A lifetime sports junkie, Wubbels considers working with Tom Lehman in the writing of *A Passion for the Game* to be a highlight of his literary career. Go to **www.TomLehman.com** and take a look at one of the most beautiful golf books ever published.

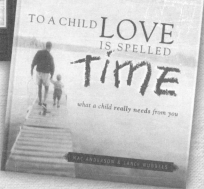

The heartwarming video for *To a Child Love Is Spelled T-I-M-E* has been sweeping through the Internet. Visit **www.BronzeBowInspiration.com** to view it and find more excellent gift books for every occasion.

UNLEASH *Your* GREATNESS

AT BRONZE BOW PUBLISHING WE ARE COMMITTED to helping you achieve your ultimate potential in functional athletic strength, fitness, natural muscular development, and all-around superb health and youthfulness.

Our books, videos, newsletters, Web sites, and training seminars will bring you the very latest in scientifically validated information that has been carefully extracted and compiled from leading scientific, medical, health, nutritional, and fitness journals worldwide.

Our goal is to empower you! To arm you with the best possible knowledge in all facets of strength and personal development so that you can make the right choices that are appropriate for *you*.

Now, as always, **the difference between greatness and mediocrity** begins with a choice. It is said that knowledge is power. But that statement is a half truth. Knowledge is power only when it has been tested, proven, and applied to your life. At that point knowledge becomes wisdom, and in wisdom there truly is *power*. The power to help you choose wisely.

So join us as we bring you the finest in health-building information and natural strength-training strategies to help you reach your ultimate potential.

FOR INFORMATION ON ALL OUR EXCITING NEW SPORTS AND FITNESS PRODUCTS, CONTACT:

BRONZE BOW PUBLISHING

2600 East 26th Street, Minneapolis, MN 55406
Toll Free: 866.724.8200
www.bronzebowpublishing.com